FIRST BUT FORGOTTEN

— THE UNTOLD STORY OF —

MARY GOLDA ROSS

PIONEERING SPACE ENGINEER

BY KATRINA M. PHILLIPS

CAPSTONE PRESS
a capstone imprint

Published by Capstone Press, an imprint of Capstone
1710 Roe Crest Drive, North Mankato, Minnesota 56003
capstonepub.com

Library of Congress Cataloging-in-Publication Data is available on the Library of Congress website.

ISBN: 9781669070030 (hardcover)
ISBN: 9781669069980 (paperback)
ISBN: 9781669069997 (ebook PDF)

Summary: You may have heard about human "computers" like Katherine Johnson who were essential to NASA's space program. But there were other women who also played key roles in the Space Race—like Cherokee engineer Mary Golda Ross who became Lockheed Martin's first female engineer and later worked on projects with NASA. Uncover Ross's story and her contributions to NASA's space program.

Editorial Credits
Editor: Ericka Smith; Designer: Sarah Bennett; Media Researcher: Svetlana Zhurkin; Production Specialist: Katy LaVigne

Image Credits
Getty Images: Corbis, 11, Corbis/Dick Whittington Studio, 15, Howard R. Hollem, 10, Hulton Archive, 13, PhotoQuest/Office of War Information, 14, U.S. Air Force, 23; Library of Congress: 6, Walter Smalling Jr., 9; NASA: 17, 19, 20, Bob Nye, 21, Japan Aerospace Exploration Agency/Koichi Wakata, 29; Newscom: Picture History, 7, Pictures From History, cover, 5, SIPA/PAJIC, 25; Shutterstock: Jose Luis Stephens, 28, Julia Khimich (background), cover (right) and throughout, Nadegda Rozova (background), cover (left) and throughout; The Smithsonian Institution: National Museum of the American Indian, "Mary Golda Ross: Ad Astra Per Astra" by America Meredith (Cherokee Nation), catalog number 26/8630, 27

Direct Quotations
Page 4, from Summer 2003, *Prologue* article, "20 July 1969," archives.gov
Page 4, from *John F. Kennedy Presidential Library and Museum* webpage, "Address at Rice University on the Nation's Space Effort," jfklibrary.org
Page 21, from *NASA* webpage, "Katherine Johnson Biography," nasa.gov
Page 28, from Feb. 11, 2022, *National Air and Space Museum* article, "Mary Golda Ross: Aerospace Engineer, Educator, and Advocate," airandspace.si.edu
Page 29, from Oct. 6, 2022, *Smithsonian* article, "Nicole Mann Becomes the First Native American Woman in Space," smithsonianmag.com

Printed and bound in the USA. 5853

TABLE OF CONTENTS

Words in **bold** are in the glossary.

INTRODUCTION

PUTTING A MAN ON THE MOON

It was July 20, 1969. More than 600 million people watched as astronaut Neil Armstrong set foot on the moon. "That's one small step for man," Armstrong said, "one giant leap for mankind." The United States had beaten the Soviet Union in the Space Race.

Seven years earlier, in September 1962, President Kennedy delivered a famous speech about going to the moon. "We choose to go to the moon in this decade and do the other things, not because they are easy, but because they are hard," Kennedy proclaimed.

Kennedy was right. It wasn't easy. It would take thousands of people to help the United States send a man to the moon and bring him back safely.

One of those people was a Cherokee woman from Oklahoma named Mary Golda Ross. She was an **engineer** who had spent years working on technology for space exploration. Her groundbreaking—and top-secret—work would help change history.

CHAPTER ONE

GROWING UP CHEROKEE

Mary Golda Ross was born on August 9, 1908, in Park Hill, Oklahoma. She was a descendant of the Cherokee principal chief John Ross. He had led his people through the Trail of Tears in the 1830s.

Cherokee people valued education. They knew that girls as well as boys deserved the best education possible. When she was a little girl, Ross's parents sent her to live with her grandparents in Tahlequah, Oklahoma, so that she could receive a good education.

John Ross

Cherokee Removal and the Trail of Tears

The United States government had forced the Cherokee to leave their beloved homelands in what is now the state of Georgia and march west to **Indian Territory**. Thousands of Cherokee people died along this Trail of Tears. Once they reached Indian Territory, the Cherokee had to rebuild their lives. They built new houses and schools, and they rebuilt their government.

The Cherokee people during their forced move to Indian Territory

Ross started taking classes at the Northeastern State Teachers College when she was only 16 years old. She graduated with a degree in mathematics in 1928. After graduation, she taught mathematics and science classes during the **Great Depression**.

Ross also took graduate classes at Colorado State College of Education every summer. She eventually earned a master's degree in mathematics. She also took every astronomy course they offered.

In 1936, Ross started working for the Bureau of Indian Affairs. The next year, she was sent to work at a federal Indian **boarding school** in New Mexico.

But the nation would soon find itself in the midst of war. And Ross's mathematical training would help the United States and its allies win World War II (1939–1945).

A building at Northeastern State University that was once part of Northeastern State Teachers College

CHAPTER TWO

JOINING THE WAR EFFORT

World War II started in 1939 when Germany invaded Poland. The United States entered the war after the December 1941 bombing of Pearl Harbor in Hawaii. The U.S. joined Great Britain and the Soviet Union as the key nations in what would be called the Allied forces.

Men and women across the United States joined the war effort. Men enlisted in the military. More than 350,000 women also joined the military. Thousands more helped fill men's absences at workplaces.

A woman works on a bomber plane in 1942.

But the nation needed more than soldiers and sailors. It needed machinery and technology to win the war, and for that it needed mathematicians and engineers. In 1941, Ross's father suggested that she move to California to look for work. In 1942, Lockheed Aircraft Corporation hired Ross as a mathematical research assistant.

Indigenous Participation in WWII

More than 45,000 **Indigenous** people served in the military during WWII, including about 800 women. They served in the Women's Army Corps (WAC) and the Women Accepted for Volunteer Emergency Service (WAVES). Others worked as nurses.

In 1943, an estimated 12,000 Native women worked in the war industries. While many took war jobs away from their reservations, those who stayed on their reservations took over jobs that had been held by men.

Indigenous women at a military base in North Carolina in 1943

The Allies needed as many fast fighter planes as they could get. Lockheed's P-38 Lightning fighter plane was one of the fastest. It was the first plane that could travel more than 400 miles (644 kilometers) per hour.

But there were a lot of issues with the P-38. Lockheed's wind tunnels couldn't reach the speed of the plane in flight, so pilots had to test the planes in the air. An expert test pilot named Ralph Virden died during a practice run in 1941. Other test pilots had trouble maintaining control of the plane.

Two Lockheed P-38 Lightning aircraft in flight

Workers assembling P-38 Lightning fighter planes in 1943

There were no computers in the 1940s like we have today. But there were human "computers"—women like Ross whose mathematical skills helped fix dangerous problems like the P-38's issues. Ross and the other researchers worked around the clock to find a solution.

Lockheed was so impressed with Ross's work that they sent her to the University of California, Los Angeles (UCLA), after the war to earn a certification in **aeronautical** engineering. She finished the coursework in 1949 and was the first Indigenous woman to earn the certification. After completing the program, she officially became Lockheed's first female engineer in 1950. But Ross's work with Lockheed was just beginning.

The UCLA campus around 1950

CHAPTER THREE

A SECRET MISSION

While Ross was earning her certification at UCLA, another war was on the horizon. The **Cold War** began a few years after the end of World War II. The United States and the Soviet Union had been allies during the war, but growing disagreements between the two countries changed their relationship. Both nations were working on nuclear weapons, and their rush to build these weapons spilled over into a race to get to outer space.

The United States government turned to the National Aeronautics and Space Administration (NASA). Its scientists and engineers would be on the front lines of the Space Race. But they couldn't do it alone. Engineers who worked at companies like Lockheed had helped the country win World War II. Now the country needed their skills to win another war.

A researcher working on engine systems for an agency that would later become NASA

In 1953, Lockheed pulled its 40 top engineers into a secret project. Ross was the only woman in the group. She was also the only Indigenous person on the team. Known by the code name "Skunk Works," this group worked on developing **satellites** and plans for space travel.

Ross also worked with NASA. She was part of the Agena Target Vehicle project. The *Agena* was an unmanned spacecraft that helped NASA practice space maneuvers and docking techniques. This was part of Project Gemini—NASA's second human spaceflight program. The project's goal was to test out equipment, procedures, and skills needed to send a person to the moon.

FACT The spacecraft and techniques tested during Project Gemini helped NASA prepare for the Apollo program—the program that sent Americans to the moon. Without the engineers' work on Gemini, the Apollo missions would never have happened.

Testing of the *Agena* (left) and the *Gemini 6* spacecraft (right) in 1952

The engineers who worked on spaceflight projects often started with **missiles** and other things that were first designed for military purposes. This was the case for the Agena Target Vehicle project.

For this project, Ross worked on the spacecraft's "orbital dynamics." She calculated the **transfer orbit** as the **rocket** left Earth's atmosphere. Today, engineers use computer programs to calculate these numbers.

Ross also helped write one of NASA's handbooks about space travel to other planets in the solar system.

The launch of the *Agena* in 1966

Katherine Johnson and NASA's Human Computers

Women like Ross used their math and engineering skills as if they were human "computers." A Black woman named Katherine Johnson (1918–2020) took a job as a mathematician at what's now known as NASA in 1953. She calculated the trajectory, or path, for the 1961 space mission that sent the first American to space. She also calculated the launch window, the time period during which a spacecraft must be launched, for the 1961 Mercury mission.

In 1962, NASA decided to use electronic computers to make calculations for the mission that sent astronaut John Glenn into orbit around Earth. But Glenn refused to fly unless Johnson confirmed the computer's calculations. "If she says they're good," Glenn said, "then I'm ready to go."

Johnson working for NASA in 1966

Johnson also helped with calculations for the 1969 Apollo 11 mission.

But that wasn't all Ross did at Lockheed. She worked on the Poseidon and Trident missiles. These were missiles that could be launched by submarines. She also worked on reentry vehicles for missiles for the Polaris project. Reentry vehicles returned missiles to Earth after reaching space.

Ross retired from Lockheed in 1973 as a senior engineer. Throughout her career, she had received a number of honors and awards for her work.

A Polaris missile launched from a U.S. submarine during a test in 1960

CHAPTER FOUR

A LASTING LEGACY

Ross didn't stop working when she retired from Lockheed. Like her Cherokee ancestors, she recognized the power of education. She toured the country giving speeches about the importance of education. She worked to make mathematics and engineering more welcoming for women and for Indigenous people.

In 2004, Ross learned about a new museum—the National Museum of the American Indian in Washington, DC. Ross was invited to participate in an event called the Native Nations Procession. She was very excited. Ross asked her niece to make Ross's first traditional Cherokee dress for the event. She couldn't believe how many people had come to celebrate the opening of the museum.

Indigenous people during the Native Nations Procession in Washington, DC, in 2004

FACT More than 25,000 Indigenous people from more than 500 Indigenous nations participated in the 2004 Native Nations Procession. They had come from the United States, Canada, Mexico, Central America, and South America.

Ross died on April 29, 2008, in Los Altos, California, a few months before what would have been her 100th birthday.

We still don't know everything Ross did at Lockheed. A lot of her work is considered classified information. That means that it is too important to be shared with the general public. But we do know that she helped the nation reach one of its biggest goals—sending American astronauts to space and putting a man on the moon.

FACT In 2019, Ross was featured on a one-dollar coin. It honored her contributions to NASA's space program.

A painting of Ross by Cherokee artist America Meredith
at the National Museum of the American Indian

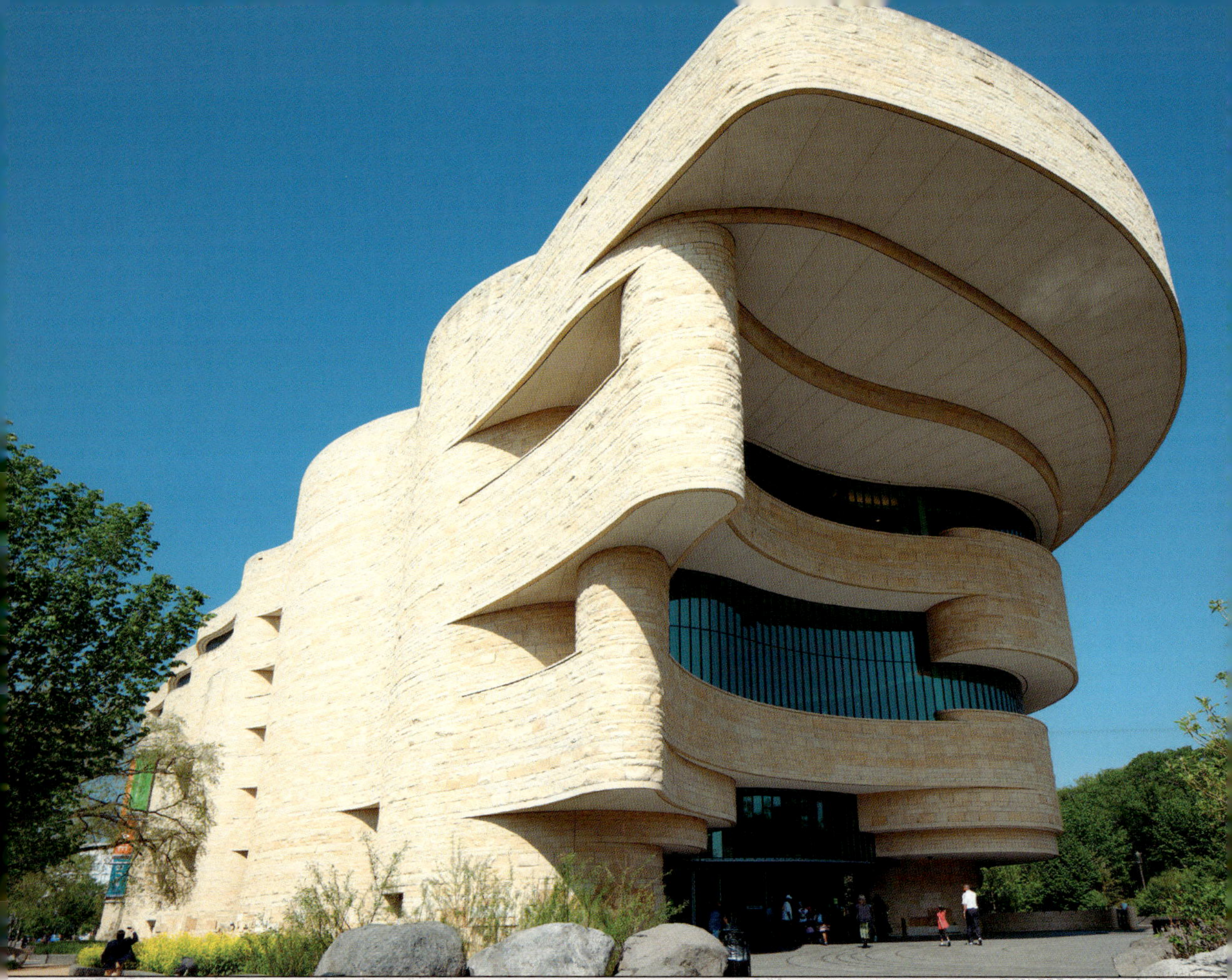

The National Museum of the American Indian
in Washington, DC

Ross was proud of her work, and she was proud to be Cherokee. When she died, she left $400,000 to the National Museum of the American Indian. She wanted to help the museum tell the true stories of Indigenous people—"not just the story of the past," she explained, "but an ongoing story."

In 2022, another Indigenous woman made space history. Nicole Mann (Wailacki) became the first Indigenous woman to go to space when she and the crew of the *Endurance* headed for the International Space Station. Mann's flight came 20 years after John Herrington became the first Indigenous person to go to space. Mann took a dreamcatcher from her mother on the journey. "I feel very proud," she said before liftoff.

Mary Golda Ross may have kept her feet on the ground. But her life's work created a path for other Indigenous men and women to follow their dreams of reaching the stars.

NASA astronaut Mann aboard the International Space Station

GLOSSARY

aeronautical (air-oh-NAHT-uh-kuhl)—relating to the science of flight

boarding school (BOR-ding SKOOL)—federal schools that were designed to erase Indigenous languages, cultures, and ways of life. Children were often forcibly removed from their families and communities and sent to boarding schools.

Cold War (KOHLD WOR)—a conflict between the United States and the Soviet Union that lasted from about 1947 to 1991

engineer (en-juh-NEER)—someone trained to design and build machines, vehicles, bridges, roads, or other structures

Great Depression (GRAYT di-PRESH-uhn)—a period of hard times in the U.S. from 1929 to 1939; many people lost their jobs

Indian Territory (IN-dee-uhn TER-uh-tor-ee)—land west of the Mississippi River the U.S. government reserved for Indigenous nations that were forcibly removed from their homelands

Indigenous (in-DIJ-uh-nuhss)—of the people who have lived in a place from the beginning or before colonists or settlers

missile (MISS-uhl)—an object that is thrown, shot, or launched as a weapon

rocket (ROK-it)—a vehicle usually shaped like a long tube with a pointed end; rockets move by pushing fuel from one end

satellite (SAT-uh-lite)—a spacecraft that circles Earth; satellites gather and send information to Earth

transfer orbit (TRANS-fur OR-bit)—the path that a spacecraft uses to move from one orbit to another

READ MORE

Phillips, Katrina M. *Indigenous Peoples: Women Who Made a Difference.* New York: Scholastic Inc., 2023.

Sorell, Traci. *Classified: The Secret Career of Mary Golda Ross, Cherokee Aerospace Engineer.* Minneapolis: Millbrook Press, 2021.

Thorpe, Andrea. *The Story of Katherine Johnson: A Biography Book for New Readers.* Emeryville, CA: Rockridge Press, 2021.

INTERNET SITES

Kiddle: Mary Golda Ross Facts for Kids
kids.kiddle.co/Mary_Golda_Ross

NASA: Mary Ross: A Hidden Figure
nasa.gov/image-article/mary-ross-hidden-figure

National Air and Space Museum: Mary Golda Ross: Aerospace Engineer, Educator, and Advocate
airandspace.si.edu/stories/editorial/mary-g-ross-aerospace-engineer

INDEX

ABOUT THE AUTHOR

Dr. Katrina Phillips is a citizen of the Red Cliff Band of Lake Superior Ojibwe. She earned her BA and PhD in history from the University of Minnesota, and she teaches Native American history and the history of the American West at Macalester College.